2021
Restaurants

The Food Enthusiast's
Long Weekend Guide

Andrew Delaplaine

GET 3 FREE NOVELS
Like political thrillers?
See next page to download 3 FREE page-turning
novels—no strings attached.

NO BUSINESS HAS PAID A SINGLE PENNY OR GIVEN *ANYTHING*
TO BE INCLUDED IN THIS BOOK.

Senior Writer - **James Cubby**

WANT 3 *FREE* THRILLERS?

Why, of course you do!
If you like these writers--
Vince Flynn, Brad Thor, Tom Clancy, James Patterson, David Baldacci, John Grisham, Brad Meltzer, Daniel Silva, Don DeLillo
If you like these TV series –
House of Cards, Scandal, West Wing, The Good Wife, Madam Secretary, Designated Survivor
Besides writing travel books, I've written political thrillers for

You'll love the **unputdownable** series about Jack Houston St. Clair, with political intrigue, romance, and loads of action and suspense.

many years that have delighted hundreds of thousands of readers. I want to introduce you to my work!
Send me an email and I'll send you a link where you can download the first 3 books in my bestselling series, absolutely FREE.
Mention **this book** when you email me.
andrewdelaplaine@mac.com

The Food Enthusiast's

Long Weekend Guide

Table of Contents

Introduction

What a wonderful town, Chicagoland.

I couldn't believe the place when I first saw it. I was coming from New York (back in the '70s) in fine weather in early summer. It was night. I took a cab into town and walked up the Magnificent Mile in awe. Ladies and gentlemen walked down the street arm-in-arm, actually promenading.

There was grass on Michigan Avenue. Real grass. I reached down and touched it. You wouldn't find grass like that on Fifth Avenue. No, sir.

There was an electricity in the air in Chicago I noticed that very first night. And I've always been aware of it. There's that same sense in New York, of course, a sensation of excitement, of swiftness, of opportunity—*of hustle*—but somehow it was different here in Chicago. The pace here has slightly less of an edge to it. The people are nicer. They are polite. They are not rude, crude or rough. Maybe the word I'm looking for is *Normal.* It's that Midwest upbringing, I tell myself, and that must be it. This may be the City of Big Shoulders, but the people inhabiting it are as nice as the farmers plowing fields 300 miles away. (Well, there are certain neighborhoods....)

That first night I spent sleeping on the floor of our branch office at the corner of Oak and Rush, which I found out later was quite an exciting corner with a fascinating history. When I woke up in the morning and looked out of the floor-to-ceiling windows, I saw people swimming in the lake.

Swimming!

In the lake. In the 1970s!

I was aghast.

Back in New York, you wouldn't dip your toe in the Hudson River or the East River.

That was then. This is now. Now they're harvesting oysters from beds in the East River.

I remember running down and asking a cop how people could swim in the filthy water. He explained that the river flowing into the lake had been reversed. The river flowed *backwards!* The water was clean.

I couldn't believe it.

But this was just the beginning of a long love affair with Chicago. There's nothing not to like about this town—except the freezing wind that comes off the lake in the wintertime.

A couple of years later, in February, I was having a business lunch at the top of the **Hancock Tower** in what is now called the **Signature Room**. A blizzard blew snow off the lake so hard the snow moved horizontally, not vertically. Looking over the shoulder of the person opposite me, I saw the building swaying. I didn't know if the Hancock Tower was swaying or the building I was looking at. I am not an engineer. I just knew this was no place for a Southern boy.

After lunch, my head bent down, I made my way back to my office and announced to the staff that the Editorial Department of our travel magazine (that would be me) was moving to our offices in Miami, at least for the winter months.

I've returned dozens of times, of course—even in February—and the simple truth is that whether it's winter, summer, spring or fall, there's no place like this Toddlin' Town.

Before we get into the nitty-gritty, I'm reprinting Carl Sanders's famous poem "Chicago," first published I think in 1914. It captures the city like no other verse ever written.

HOG Butcher for the World,
    Tool Maker, Stacker of Wheat,
    Player with Railroads and the Nation's Freight Handler;
    Stormy, husky, brawling,
    City of the Big Shoulders:
    They tell me you are wicked and I believe them, for
    I have seen your painted women under the gas lamps
        luring the farm boys.

And they tell me you are crooked and I answer: Yes,
it
    is true I have seen the gunman kill and go free to
    kill again.
And they tell me you are brutal and my reply is: On
the
    faces of women and children I have seen the marks
    of wanton hunger.
And having answered so I turn once more to those
who
    sneer at this my city, and I give them back the
sneer
    and say to them:
Come and show me another city with lifted head
singing
    so proud to be alive and coarse and strong and
cunning.
Flinging magnetic curses amid the toil of piling job
on
    job, here is a tall bold slugger set vivid against the
    little soft cities;
Fierce as a dog with tongue lapping for action,
cunning
    as a savage pitted against the wilderness,
        Bareheaded,
        Shoveling,
        Wrecking,
        Planning,
        Building, breaking, rebuilding,
Under the smoke, dust all over his mouth, laughing
with
    white teeth,
Under the terrible burden of destiny laughing as a

young
man laughs,
Laughing even as an ignorant fighter laughs who has
never lost a battle,
Bragging and laughing that under his wrist is the
pulse.
and under his ribs the heart of the people,
Laughing!
Laughing the stormy, husky, brawling laughter of
Youth, half-naked, sweating, proud to be Hog
Butcher, Tool Maker, Stacker of Wheat, Player
with
Railroads and Freight Handler to the Nation.

There are so many different worlds in Chicago.
There are the edgier sections of Pilsen and Logan
Square, the old city center in the Loop, the dramatic

sweep of buildings along the Gold Coast fronting a beach that in summertime looks almost like it doesn't belong here, the Puerto Rican barrios of Humboldt Park and Devon Avenue, the elegant areas around Hyde Park, the craziness of Boystown, the world-class shopping along the Magnificent Mile, the theatre scene that's second only to what you'll find in New York, a music scene that's among the most vibrant in the country, you will find it almost impossible to absorb all this glorious city has to offer over a Long Weekend.

But you will get a taste so thrilling that you'll want to return again and again.

The A to Z Listings
Ridiculously Extravagant
Sensible Alternatives
Quality Bargain Spots

ALINEA
1723 N Halsted St, 312-867-0110
www.alinearestaurant.com
CUISINE: American (New)/European
DRINKS: Wine
SERVING: Dinner
PRICE RANGE: $$$$
NEIGHBORHOOD: Lincoln Park
Foodies love this small two-level eatery with each
floor offering a different dining experience. The
atmosphere is not 'fun,' but severely elegant in a most

restrained way. You might even call it austere. (I've had more fun in church, sad to say.) If you don't take food as seriously as they do, stay away. Unique dishes are more like art creations, menu changes often. "The Kitchen Table" gets you into a room with just the chef & waiters. 6 people only. Expensive. Then there are 2 prix-fixe menus, the "Gallery" with 16-to-18 courses served on the ground floor, and the "Salon" menu, served upstairs, which has 10-12 courses. Check current (very high) prices, and plan on spending the whole evening there. Favorites: Wagyu beef and Asian street food. Excellent wine pairings.

ANN SATHER
909 W Belmont Ave, Chicago, 773-348-2378
www.annsather.com
CUISINE: Scandinavian
DRINKS: No Booze
SERVING: Breakfast, Brunch
PRICE RANGE: $$
NEIGHBORHOOD: Lakeview
One of several scattered throughout Chicago, this Swedish eatery serves up one of the best breakfasts in town. Menu favorites include: Swedish Breakfast and once you taste one of their fresh-baked cinnamon rolls, you'll rave about them too.

ARBOR
2545 W Diversey Ave, Chicago, 312-866-0795
www.arborprojects.com
CUISINE: American (New)
DRINKS: Full Bar
SERVING: Breakfast & Lunch; closed Sat & Sun

PRICE RANGE: $$
NEIGHBORHOOD: Logan Square
Industrial kitchen and coffeehouse serving breakfast
& lunch only. Menu picks: Breakfast burrito and
Rhubarb oatmeal. Wine pairings and crafted
cocktails. Daily specials.

ARCADIA
1639 S Wabash Ave, Chicago, 312-360-9500
www.acadiachicago.com
CUISINE: American
DRINKS: Full Bar
SERVING: Dinner
PRICE RANGE: $$$$
NEIGHBORHOOD: Near Southside/South Loop
Run by Chef Ryan McCaskey, this high-end eatery
offers a creative menu featuring dishes like Lobster
potpie and Black cod. If you're a meat lover, try the
Wagu tri-tip, a meat and potatoes dish with thick
slices of beef. Desserts are just as interesting and
delicious especially the chocolate pudding that's

filled with pieces of sponge cake, hazelnuts, and almond-cookie shards. The bar serves novel cocktails and offers a nice wine list. The décor is simple but comfortable. Closed Monday and Tuesday.

ARTOPOLIS BAKERY & CAFE
306 S Halsted St, Chicago, 312-559-9000
www.artopolischicago.com
CUISINE: Greek
DRINKS: Full Bar
SERVING: Brunch, Lunch, Dinner
PRICE RANGE: $$
NEIGHBORHOOD: Near West Side
A combination bakery, café, bar and retail shop. Here you'll find fresh baked Greek pastries like their signature "artopitas." Their menu features a selection of soups, salads, wood-fired pizzas and sandwiches made with hearth-baked bread. Traditional Greek dishes like eggplant moussaka and roasted leg of lamb are also offered. In the shop you'll find breads and pastries, gift baskets, chocolates, olive oils and vinegars.

ATWOOD CAFÉ

1 W Washington St, Chicago, 312-368-1900
www.atwoodrestaurant.com
CUISINE: American
DRINKS: Full Bar
SERVING: Breakfast, Lunch, Dinner
PRICE RANGE: $$$
NEIGHBORHOOD: The Loop
Located in the historic Reliance Building along with
the **Hotel Burnham**, this restaurant offers classic
American cuisine served in an Art Deco decorated
dining room that features 18-foot-tall windows. Chef
Derek Simcik's menu features dishes made with
fresh, seasonal ingredients. Menu favorites include:
Roasted chicken and Vegetable pot pie. Great choice
for pre-theater nosh.

AU CHEVAL

800 W Randolph St, Chicago, 312-929-4580
www.auchevalchicago.com
CUISINE: American (New)
DRINKS: Full Bar
SERVING: Lunch, Dinner
PRICE RANGE: $$
NEIGHBORHOOD: West Loop
Upscale diner-style eatery with an open kitchen.
Great varied menu but they are famous for their
burgers. Menu picks: Honey-fried chicken and
Cheeseburger. Usually a wait since there's limited
seating.

AVEC
615 W Randolph St, Chicago, 312-377-2002
www.avecrestaurant.com
CUISINE: French/Mediterranean
DRINKS: Full Bar
SERVING: Lunch & Dinner
PRICE RANGE: $$$
NEIGHBORHOOD: Near West Side
This intimate restaurant offers a small plate menu and communal seating. Menu favorites include Ricotta flatbread, Pork shoulder and Papperdelle. No reservations – which means there's often a wait. Now serving brunch.

BAD HUNTER
802 W Randolph St, Chicago, 312-265-1745
www.badhunter.com
CUISINE: American (New)
DRINKS: Full bar
SERVING: Lunch & Dinner
PRICE RANGE: $$
NEIGHBORHOOD: Near West Side, West Loop
Hip restaurant with a vegetable-focused menu. Favorites: Smoked salmon tartine and Butternut Squash sandwich. Bar serves low-alcohol craft cocktails.

BAKERY AT FAT RICE
2951 W Diversey Ave, Chicago, 773-661-9544
www.eatfatrice.com
CUISINE: Bakery
DRINKS: No Booze
SERVING: Breakfast, Lunch; closed Mon & Tues

PRICE RANGE: $$
NEIGHBORHOOD: Logan Square
Eclectic bakery that also serves breakfast & lunch.
Portuguese-style sweet dough has baked into it
Vienna all-beef hot dog, hot sport peppers, chopped
onion, tomato and then topped with poppy & celery
seeds and spread with Chinese mustard. Wow.
There's a great Char siu pineapple bun filled with
BBQ pork.

BERGHOFF
17 W Adams St, Chicago, 312-427-3170
www.theberghoff.com
CUISINE: German
DRINKS: Full Bar
SERVING: Lunch, Dinner
PRICE RANGE: $$
NEIGHBORHOOD: The Loop
A Chicago landmark, this restaurant serves German-
style cuisine offering a variety of appetizers, salads,
sandwiches, and entrees including vegetarian and
gluten-free dishes. But gluten-free is not what you
come here for. It's that big juicy Reuben on rye that is

hard to hold in two hands. Menu favorites include: Weiner Schnitzel and Jagerschnitzel - Pork Cutlet, with mushrooms and bacon. Good selection of German beer and lagers.

BIG JONES
5347 N Clark St, 773-275-5725
www.bigjoneschicago.com
CUISINE: Southern
DRINKS: Full Bar
SERVING: Lunch & Dinner, Weekend Brunch
PRICE RANGE: $$
NEIGHBORHOOD: Andersonville
Modern style eatery with a nice little bar area up front before it turns into a long narrow room with tables on either side. Very simple but comfortable. There's a fenced-in patio out back that's nice in good weather. Serves Southern-style cooking from New Orleans and the Carolina Lowcountry. Favorites: Cajun Boudin Balls (breaded liver sausage); Rutabaga Bisque (I know, but trust me—it's delicious); Crispy Catfish (with a unique corn and rice flour breading I hadn't seen in many years); Gumbo Ya-Ya (very strong Cajun elements—very nice) and Barbecued Pork Shoulder (smoked with pecan wood). The fried chicken is also very highly recommended—they cook it in lard and ham drippings. (Bring a Lipitor!) Back patio available weather permitting.

BIG STAR
1531 N Damen, (bet. Wicker Park Ave & Pierce Ave), Chicago, 773-235-4039
www.bigstarchicago.com

CUISINE: Mexican, Tex-Mex
DRINKS: Full Bar
SERVING: Lunch, Dinner & Late Night
PRICE RANGE: $$
NEIGHBORHOOD: Wicker Park
Nice range of Mexican food, from fish, chicken and beef tacos, to a Sonoran Hot Dag (a bacon-wrapped hot dog with pinto beans, lime mayo, mustard, onions and Big Star hot sauce on a bolillo roll). Most people don't know it, but Big Star has blended 20+ signature barrels of whiskey with some of Kentucky's best distilleries, creating perhaps the biggest single-barrel selection in the U.S. If you like American whiskey, you MUST put a stop here at the top of your list.

BILLY GOAT TAVERN
430 N Michigan Ave (Lower Level), Chicago, 312-222-1525
www.billygoattavern.com
CUISINE: American, Burgers
DRINKS: Full Bar
SERVING: Lunch & Dinner

PRICE RANGE: $
NEIGHBORHOOD: Near North Side
Located underneath the Chicago Tribune Building, this tavern offers a genuine diner/soda fountain feel. Worth a stop if you're in the neighborhood but other than that the burgers aren't that impressive. Locations all over the city.

BLACKBIRD
619 W Randolph St, Chicago, 312-715-0708
www.blackbirdrestaurant.com
CUISINE: American
DRINKS: Full Bar
SERVING: Lunch & Dinner
PRICE RANGE: $$$
NEIGHBORHOOD: Near West Side
They can claim Michelin stars here since 2011, and the cooks here (sorry, chefs) have more James Beard Awards than you can shake a stick at. I find the décor to be antiseptic and clinically sleek and modern, to the point that the bar looks like a big white slab on which a medical examiner might conduct an autopsy. It's about as warm and fuzzy and charming in here as a meat locker. But if you look past the studied modernity of the setting, you'll love the food: roasted chicken roulade, hanger steak with rutabaga (I love rutabaga, and you so seldom see it offered), wood-grilled sturgeon with roasted leeks, sucking pig served with risotto (dinner only), poached turbot (the most delicate I've had in a long time), and the aged duck breast, simply outstanding.

CAFÉ MARIE- JEANNE

1001 N California Ave, Chicago,773-904-7660
www.cafe-marie-jeanne.com
CUISINE: French
DRINKS: Full Bar
SERVING: Breakfast, Lunch, & Dinner; closed Tues
PRICE RANGE: $$
NEIGHBORHOOD: West Town, Humboldt Park
Cozy French café with a deli counter. Menu is a la
cart. One favorite is their Avocado toast with
raspberry vinaigrette jam. Or the bursting-with-flavor
duck frites. Or the calf brains served on brioche toast.
Great selection of wines, craft beers and liquors. Top-
notch brunch.

CELLAR DOOR PROVISIONS

3025 W Diversey Ave, Chicago, 773-697-8337
www.cellardoorprovisions.com
CUISINE: American (New)
DRINKS: Full Bar
SERVING: Breakfast, Lunch (till 3) Wed-Sun;
Dinner till 9 on Fri-Sat; Closed Mon & Tues
PRICE RANGE: $$
NEIGHBORHOOD: Logan Square
Low-key neighborhood eatery offering a simple but
exquisitely prepared menu. They have the best bread
in town, with croissants that have a flakiness that will
surprise and please you. Decadent quiche. The ash-
wood chairs and Spartan tables are about as basic as
you can get, but that doesn't matter. Light streams in
from the high windows on the street. While it's a
perfect place for breakfast or lunch, on the 2 nights
they served their very reasonably priced prix fixe

dinner, you get a four-course meal you won't soon forget. Items like corn soup, plum salad, roasted peaches. Nice choice for brunch. Lots of vegetable-focused dishes with international ingredients.

CESAR'S RESTAURANT
3166 N Clark St, Chicago, 773-248-2835
www.killermargaritas.com/eat.html
CUISINE: Mexican
DRINKS: Full Bar
SERVING: Dinner
PRICE RANGE: $$
NEIGHBORHOOD: Lakeview
This Mexican restaurant serves delicious authentic Mexican fare and is known for its lip-smacking margaritas. Check out their website for special events like Cinco de Mayo and Pride Parade. Good food and friendly service. (Try the Peach margaritas.)

THE CHICAGO CHOP HOUSE
60 W Ontario St, Chicago, 312-787-7100
www.chicagochophouse.com
CUISINE: Steakhouse
DRINKS: Full Bar
SERVING: Dinner
PRICE RANGE: $$$$
NEIGHBORHOOD: Near North Side
Located in a century-old Victorian, this place serves Mishima Ranch Wagyu Beef and is one of the best steakhouses in the city. Menu includes their famous 64-ounce porterhouse steak with a pretty good list of wines by the glass. Portraits of old Chicago gangsters (lots of those to choose from, including a few

politicians) hang on the wall and the clientele is filled with regulars who are serious about their steaks.

THE CHICAGO DINER
3411 N Halsted St, Chicago, 773-935-6696
www.veggiediner.com
CUISINE: Vegetarian, Vegan
DRINKS: Beer & Wine Only
SERVING: Lunch, Dinner
PRICE RANGE: $$
NEIGHBORHOOD: Lakeview
A landmark vegetarian/vegan diner that has been serving good food for more than 20 years. Comfort food with a vegetarian twist. Menu favorites include: Portobello mushroom burgers and a Nacho appetizer. Yummy desserts. Even if you think you hate vegan food, give this place a try. As Lucille Ball said about

Vitameatavegamin in that famous commercial, "It's so tasty, too!"

COALFIRE PIZZA
1321 W Grand Ave, Chicago, 312-226-2625
www.coalfirechicago.com
CUISINE: Pizza
DRINKS: Beer & Wine
SERVING: Lunch, Dinner
PRICE RANGE: $$
NEIGHBORHOOD: Near West Side
Here you'll find an American version of the traditional Neapolitan style pizza made in an 800-degree clean burning coal oven.

CITY MOUSE
Ace Hotel
311 N Morgan St, Chicago, 312-764-1908
www.citymousechicago.com
CUISINE: American (New)
DRINKS: Full Bar
SERVING: Breakfast, Lunch, & Dinner
PRICE RANGE: $$
NEIGHBORHOOD: Fulton Market, West Loop, Near West Side
Comfortable eatery offering a menu of New American fare. One favorite is their goat cheese gnudi with braised lamb shank. Or the green curry with butternut squash and king crab. Or Chinese broccoli with roasted San Marzano tomatoes. A lot of the veggies served here are grown in the Ace Hotel's garden operated by Roof Crop. Daily brunch is served. Craft cocktails. Gluten-free options.

CORRIDOR BREWERY & PROVISIONS
3446 N Southport, Chicago, 773-270-4272
www.corridorchicago.com
CUISINE: American (New)
DRINKS: Full Bar
SERVING: Lunch & Dinner
PRICE RANGE: $$
NEIGHBORHOOD: Lakeview
Located in the center of the Southport Corridor, this Farmhouse craft brewery and restaurant offers a menu of Midwestern favorites like sandwiches and artisan pizzas. Beers available only in the brewery.

DRYHOP BREWERS
3155 N Broadway St, Chicago, 773-857-3155
www.dryhopchicago.com
CUISINE: American (New)
DRINKS: Full Bar
SERVING: Lunch & Dinner
PRICE RANGE: $$
NEIGHBORHOOD: Lakeview
Combination brewery and kitchen with a focus on the brews. Menu features simple shared plates of comfort food. Menu picks: Fried chicken sandwich and mac n cheese. New beer selections weekly.

DUSEK'S
1227 W 18th St, Chicago, 312-526-3851
www.dusekschicago.com
CUISINE: American
DRINKS: Full Bar
SERVING: Dinner
PRICE RANGE: $$
NEIGHBORHOOD: Pilsen
More than a bar, this place has become a popular eatery. Menu favorites include: Boneless Duck wings, Red Snapper Crudo, and Juicy Lucy burger. A dessert favorite is the chocolate bar, served with a knife and fork as it's served on a bed of marshmallow fluff and caramel drizzle. When you leave visit the Punch Bar downstairs for one of their specialty punches.

ELSKE
1350 W Randolph St, Chicago, 312-733-1314
www.elskerestaurant.com
CUISINE: American (New)

DRINKS: Full Bar
SERVING: Dinner; closed Mon & Tues
PRICE RANGE: $$$$
NEIGHBORHOOD: Near West Side, West Loop
Comfortable eatery with an affordable tasting menu.
Enjoy cocktails by the fireplace outside. Prix fixe
menu with wine pairings is quite popular. Favorites:
Confit maitakes with creamed barley and Fermented
black bean agnolotti with morels. The sweets on offer
here are particularly delectable.

FAT RICE
2957 W Diversey Ave, Chicago, 773-661-9170
www.eatfatrice.com
CUISINE: Asian Fusion/Chinese
DRINKS: Full Bar
SERVING: Lunch & Dinner; Lunch only on Sun;
Closed Mon
PRICE RANGE: $$
NEIGHBORHOOD: Logan Square
Rustic style eatery where you eat on communal tables
with an open kitchen. The place is decorated with
items picked up on trips the owners have made to far-
flung locales, very nice, comfortable and homey. The
cuisine here emphasis dishes from the Macau area
(those of you good with geography will know that
Macau was once a Portuguese colony). Besides the
Macanese food, the menu features Asian inspired
comfort food and also some Portuguese dishes. Menu
picks: Sichuan-style bacon (with bacon they smoke
in-house, wood ear mushrooms and 5-spice powder),
Pork Chop Bun and Piri-Piri Chicken, Sichuan
eggplant pickles; Potstickers; arroz gordo (fat rice)

with salted duck, roast pork, littleneck clams, and Portuguese chicken.

FLORIOLE CAFÉ & BAKERY
1220 W Webster Ave, Chicago, 773-883-1313
www.floriole.com
CUISINE: Bakery/Cafe
DRINKS: No Booze
SERVING: Breakfast/Lunch
PRICE RANGE: $$
NEIGHBORHOOD: Lincoln Park
Bakery and café serving a variety of fresh pastries. The upstairs dining room is particularly nice when the weather is clean and the sun bursts through the windows. Small menu of soups, salads, and quiches. Friday night is Pizza Night. Of course the coffee's great.

FRONTERA GRILL
445 N Clark St, Chicago, 312-661-1434
www.fronterakitchens.com
CUISINE: Mexican

DRINKS: Full Bar
SERVING: Lunch, Dinner
PRICE RANGE: $$$
NEIGHBORHOOD: Near North Side
Open since 1987, the popularity of this Mexican grill can probably be credited to Celebrity Chef and winner of Top Chef Masters Rick Bayless. The ever-changing menu features Mexican classics like enchiladas, mole and flautas. Menu favorites include: Oyster & Ceviche Combo and Carne Asada (Rib steak, bean and sweet plantain with a little bit of guac).

GALIT
2429 N Lincoln Ave, 773-360-8755
www.galitrestaurant.com
CUISINE: Middle Eastern/Mediterranean/Vegetarian
DRINKS: Full Bar
SERVING: Dinner, Closed Mondays
PRICE RANGE: $$
NEIGHBORHOOD: Lincoln Park
Hip Middle Eastern eatery with a few kitchen-side seats if you want to watch while the cooks do their thing. Otherwise, tables against the walls provide more privacy. Offering regular & shared menus. Favorites: Brisket Hummus (among several you can choose from); Carrots grilled are very flavorful, as are all of the veggie choices here; Falafel (mango, labneh, pickled turnips); Beets with black garlic; Chick thigh with crispy skin (this is really good); Balkan Stuffed Cabbage with lamb kebab. As a rule, you don't often see "creative cocktails" in a place serving this kind of food, so this is a plus. Reservations recommended.

GIANT
3209 W Armitage Ave, Chicago, 773-252-0997
www.giantrestaurant.com
CUISINE: American (New)
DRINKS: Full bar
SERVING: Dinner; closed Sun & Mon
PRICE RANGE: $$$
NEIGHBORHOOD: Logan Square
Funky restaurant set in an art decorated storefront gets its name from "Me and My Giant," a poem by Shel Silverstein who was originally from Logan Square. Cozy and casual eatery with a menu of shared dishes. The chef here takes comfort food and elevates it to something really special and unexpected. Imagine onion rings, but fried in Parmesan batter, or sweet corn fancied up with peanuts, mint and Thai chiles. Favorites: Garlic buttermilk potatoes, Happy Scallops, Chicken habanero and Sweet & sour eggplant (excellent dish you must try). Great wine selection.

GIBSONS BAR & STEAKHOUSE
1028 N Rush St (bet. Cedar St & Oak St), Chicago
312-266-8999
www.gibsonssteakhouse.com
CUISINE: Steakhouse
DRINKS: Full Bar
SERVING: Lunch, Dinner
PRICE RANGE: $$$
NEIGHBORHOOD: Near North Side
This is a very popular restaurant with traditional menu offerings of steaks, chops and seafood. The

delicious desserts are bountiful. It's busy, so book ahead.

GILT BAR
230 W Kinzie St, Chicago, 312-464-9544
www.giltbarchicago.com
CUISINE: American
DRINKS: Full Bar
SERVING: Dinner
PRICE RANGE: $$$
NEIGHBORHOOD: Near North Side, River North
Credit the recession, but a number of good mid-price but high-style restaurants have opened in Chicago in the last two years. A favorite is "Gilt Bar," a casual restaurant in the River North neighborhood that isn't casual about its cooking. The menu features New American dishes like blackened cauliflower with capers ($7) and ricotta gnocchi with sage and brown butter ($13). After dinner, head downstairs to Curio, a basement bar with a Prohibition theme. Try the

Death's Door Daisy, made with artisanal Wisconsin vodka and Aperol, a blood orange liqueur, for $10.

GIRL & THE GOAT
809 W Randolph St (bet. Green & Halsted Sts), Chicago, 312-492-6262
www.girlandthegoat.com
CUISINE: American
DRINKS: Full Bar
SERVING: Dinner
PRICE RANGE: $$$
NEIGHBORHOOD: Near West Side, West Loop
A much-blogged-about new restaurant where the "Top Chef" winner Stephanie Izard takes livestock parts seriously. The often-updated menu recently included lamb ribs with grilled avocado and pistachio piccata ($17), and braised beef tongue with masa and beef vinaigrette ($12). If you're not a carnivore, try chickpeas three ways ($11), and for dessert, potato fritters with lemon poached eggplant and Greek yogurt ($8). The soaring dining room, designed by the Chicago design firm 555 International, is warm and modern, with exposed beams, walls of charred cedar and a large open kitchen.

GOOD FORTUNE
2528 N California Ave, 773-666-5238
www.goodfortunechicago.com
CUISINE: American (New)/Mediterranean
DRINKS: Full Bar
SERVING: Dinner, Closed Mon & Tues.
PRICE RANGE: $$
NEIGHBORHOOD: Logan Square

Popular eatery in a narrow room with a bar on one side and tables on the other. Dim lighting at night creates a fun, intimate atmosphere, but it's still quite lively, not romantic and quiet. A wood-burning oven is used to prepare a lot of their dishes, and they know how to use it effectively. The menu is a bit all over the place, so you might get a Mediterranean dish followed by one from the Midwest. Favorites: Marinated beets (with fennel); Black Garlic Rigatoni; Prawns with head on served with octopus & black lentils; Roasted pork collar (from that wood-burning oven I mentioned); and a superior Ribeye with whipped celery root & bone marrow. Creative desserts and cocktails.

GT FISH & OYSTER
531 N Wells St, Chicago, 312-929-3501
www.gtoyster.com
CUISINE: Seafood / Creole / Cajun
DRINKS: Full Bar

SERVING: Lunch, Dinner
PRICE RANGE: $$$
NEIGHBORHOOD: Near North Side
This popular Cajun style seafood eatery offers an impressive small plates seasonal menu featuring a variety of fresh oysters, crab cakes, lobster rolls and calamari. Menu favorites include: Tuna pokem Oyster Po-Boy and Shrimp bruschetta. Impressive beer & wine menu.

HONKY TONK BARBEQUE
1800 S Racine Ave, Chicago, 312-226-7427
www.honkytonkbbqchicago.com
CUISINE: Barbeque
DRINKS: Full Bar
SERVING: Dinner
PRICE RANGE: $$
NEIGHBORHOOD: Pilsen
Popular hangout offering a full schedule of live music that covers the genres of American Roots music including: roaring 20s, groovy 60s; Western Swing, Honky Tonk, Rockabilly, Bluegrass, Blues, Old Time, Soul, and occasionally new age indie and rock. Menu features Championship BBQ pork, beef, chicken and other made-from-scratch dishes. This is a late night bar with theme nights like Trivia night on Wednesdays.

JAM
2853 N Kedzie Ave, Chicago, 773-292-6011
www.jamrestaurant.com
CUISINE: Breakfast, Brunch
DRINKS: Full Bar

SERVING: Breakfast, Brunch
PRICE RANGE: $$
NEIGHBORHOOD: Logan Square
While this restaurant serves both breakfast and lunch, it has earned a reputation as one of the nation's most celebrated brunch restaurants. Chef Jeffrey Mauro offers a creative menu featuring favorites like: the egg sandwich, the burrito suizo, and malted French toast.

LA SERENA CLANDESTINA
954 W Fulton Market, Chicago, 312-226-5300
www.lasirenachicago.com
CUISINE: Latin American/Brazilian
DRINKS: Full Bar
SERVING: Lunch, Dinner; closed for lunch on Sat
PRICE RANGE: $$
NEIGHBORHOOD: Fulton Market, West Loop
Cute little dining spot with a farmhouse feel. Simple menu filled with shared plate items. The standout here is the exquisite ceviche. Nice selection of wines.

LES NOMADES
222 E Ontario St, Chicago, 312-649-9010
www.lesnomades.net
CUISINE: French
DRINKS: Full Bar
SERVING: Dinner; closed Sun & Mon
PRICE RANGE: $$$$
NEIGHBORHOOD: River East
Upscale eatery located in a brownstone that throws off a lot of charm is this place that offers "French haute cuisine" and an impressive wine list (with lots of Champagnes). Menu picks: Warm lobster and

shrimp salad and Langoustine ravioli with sea scallop. For dessert they offer a variety of exceptional soufflés. Great ambiance for a romantic date.

LITTLE GOAT BREAD
820 W Randolph St, Chicago, 312-888-3455
www.littlegoatchicago.com
CUISINE: American/Bakery
DRINKS: Full Bar
SERVING: Breakfast, Lunch, Dinner
PRICE RANGE: $$
NEIGHBORHOOD: Near West Side
Celebrated Chef Stephanie Izard offers a simple menu of American favorites in this updated version of a diner with things like Shrimp & Grits and Bull's Eye French Toast. Comfortable diner-like atmosphere.

LONGMAN & EAGLE
2657 N Kedzie Ave, (bet. Milwaukee & Schubert Aves), Chicago, 773-276-7110
www.longmanandeagle.com
CUISINE: American
DRINKS: Full Bar
SERVING: Breakfast, Lunch & Dinner
PRICE RANGE: $$
NEIGHBORHOOD: Logan Square
It is a rough-edged bar that serves a refined brunch: a chunky sockeye salmon tartare with pickled mango ($10) or a wild boar "Sloppy Joe" ($10). Six hotel rooms upstairs. Logan Square, about five to six miles northwest of the Loop, is a remnant of Chicago's late-19th-century beautification movement, with a statue

of an eagle by Evelyn Longman where two of the grandest boulevards meet.

MAUDE'S LIQUOR BAR
840 W Randolph St, Chicago, 312-243-9712
www.maudesliquorbar.com
CUISINE: French
DRINKS: Full Bar
SERVING: Dinner
PRICE RANGE: $$$
NEIGHBORHOOD: Near West Side
Run by **Au Cheval** owner Brendan Sodikoff, Maude's is certainly more than a liquor bar. On the first floor there's a dining room with a marble bar and on the second there's a sunken, plush bar. Heavy on atmosphere (dimly lit with candles / exposed brick) with a nice French menu of seafood and classic

dishes. Very romantic feeling about the place. The excellent classic cocktails only enhance the experience. Menu picks: Steak tartare, Mussels, and French Onion fondue, Escargot and Gnocchi.

MI TOCAYA ANTOJERIA
2800 W Logan Blvd, Chicago, 872-315-3947
www.mitocaya.com
CUISINE: Mexican/Latin American
DRINKS: Full Bar
SERVING: Dinner; closed Mon
PRICE RANGE: $$
NEIGHBORHOOD: Logan Square
Relaxed eatery offering a menu of Mexican small plates. Favorites: Peanut butter lengua and Duck leg (carnitas style). Crispy sweetbreads are served with gremolata. Mussels come with cabbage and radishes. The steak burrito oozes with melted cheese and salty

beef. Patio dining – weather permitting. Nice selection of desserts and cocktails.

MIA FRANCESCA
3311 N Clark St, Chicago, 773-281-3310
www.miafrancesca.com
CUISINE: Italian
DRINKS: Full Bar
SERVING: Dinner
PRICE RANGE: $$
NEIGHBORHOOD: Lakeview
Popular chain restaurant in these parts serving solid if not terribly imaginative Italian fare. Noisy and crowded. Menu favorites include: Rigatoni con scarola and chicken salvia. Outdoor patio.

MOMOTARO
820 W Lake St, Chicago, 312-733-4818
www.momotarochicago.com

CUISINE: Sushi
DRINKS: Full bar
SERVING: Dinner
PRICE RANGE: $$$
NEIGHBORHOOD: Fulton Market, Near West Side, West Loop
This $3.4 million, 11,000-square-foot two-level venue is impressive in size, decoration and its giant menu (and I really mean a giant menu—it's vast). Sushi fans flock to this spot. On the ground floor they emphasize snacks and izakaya, while upstairs there's a sushi island. Favorites: Sashimi that melts in your mouth and Toro tartare. Expansive whiskey selection. Their newly acquired highball machine makes tasty cocktails like the Suntory Whisky Toki highballs with grapefruit garnish.

MONTEVERDE
1020 W Madison St, Chicago, 312-888-3041
www.monteverdechicago.com
CUISINE: Italian
DRINKS: Full Bar
SERVING: Dinner; closed Mon
PRICE RANGE: $$$
NEIGHBORHOOD: West Loop
Stylish eatery offering a menu of contemporary Italian fare. The pastas here aren't great by accident. They make it all here. There's even a mirror over the pastificio (the table where they make the pasta) so you can watch. You'll see a cook stuffing tortelli with greens and ricotta cheese before they cook it and bring it to you. Special dishes such as Grilled

octopus skewers and Duck egg ravioli. Reservations recommended.

MORRISON'S RESTAURANT AND CATERING
8127 S Ashland Ave, Chicago, 773-487-7000
https://www.allmenus.com/il/chicago/352006-morrisons-soul-food/menu/
CUISINE: Soul Food
DRINKS: No Booze
SERVING: Lunch, Dinner
PRICE RANGE: $$ / **cash only**
NEIGHBORHOOD: Auburn Gresham
Fair choice for comfort food like Mac 'n Cheese, ribs and cornbread. Daily specials. You go down a cafeteria line and point to the dishes you want. Just

like the old days. Food iso only fair, not great. Avoid
Sunday (unless you want to see everybody dressed to
the nines), because you run into the after-church
crowd. Cash only.

MOTT ST
1401 N Ashland Ave, Chicago, 773-687-9977
www.mottstreetchicago.com
CUISINE: Asian Fusion
DRINKS: Full Bar
SERVING: Dinner
PRICE RANGE: $$
NEIGHBORHOOD: Wicker Park
A lovely restaurant with an Asian street food-inspired
menu. Menu favorites include: Whiskey-marinated
pork neck, Crab Brain fried rice, and Oyster
Mushrooms. Desserts include a Choco Banana,
Mantou (yeasted doughnuts in chocolate) and Tres
Leches Cake. A great dining experience especially if
you share multiple plates.

NEXT
953 W Fulton Market, Chicago, 312-226-0858
www.nextrestaurant.com
CUISINE: Chinese/Steakhouse
DRINKS: Full Bar
SERVING: Dinner; closed Mon & Tues
PRICE RANGE: $$$$
NEIGHBORHOOD: West Loop
Upscale eatery popular among foodies who come for
Grant Achatz's unique themed tasting menus. This
dining experience completely changes every four
months. It's a very exacting place, a little on the "too

serious" side of the scale if you ask me, but if you're a diehard foodie, you'll want to put yourself through this experience. The unusual dishes here are unlike anything you've had elsewhere. This restaurant earned a James Beard Award as the Best New Restaurant in America.

NOMI
Park Hyatt Chicago
800 N Michigan Ave, Chicago, 312-239-4030
https://nomichicago.com
CUISINE: American with French influences
DRINKS: Full Bar
SERVING: Breakfast, Lunch, Dinner
PRICE RANGE: $$$$
NEIGHBORHOOD: Near North Side
It's hard to focus on the excellent food dished up here when you're glued to the captivating views from the seventh floor of the Park Hyatt Chicago, but force yourself. This elegant restaurant offers a simple menu

featuring flavorful dishes made from regionally-sourced ingredients. Menu favorites include: Seafood salad, Pork belly with escargot, braised Jamison Farms lamb and Pork secreto. Nice wine and beer list and cocktail menu.

NORTH POND RESTAURANT
2610 N Cannon Dr, Chicago, 773-477-5845
www.northpondrestaurant.com
CUISINE: American
DRINKS: Full Bar
SERVING: Dinner
PRICE RANGE: $$$$
NEIGHBORHOOD: Lincoln Park
Located within the grounds of Lincoln Park, North Pond boasts one of the loveliest settings in the city. Set in a structure built in 1912 that was originally a warming shelter for ice skaters, Chef Bruce Sherman offers a creative seasonal menu of "upscale" New American cuisine. Menu favorites include: Grilled smoke sturgeon and Grass Fed Beef. Great tasting menu. Dessert choices include: chocolate mousse and cranberry sorbet.

ORIOLE
661 W Walnut St, Chicago, 312-877-5339
www.oriolechicago.com
CUISINE: American (New)
DRINKS: Full bar
SERVING: Dinner; closed Sun & Mon
PRICE RANGE: $$$$
NEIGHBORHOOD: Near West Side, West Loop

Intimate high-end eatery that's on everyone's must-visit list, this place serves top-notch New American dishes. Favorites: Kobe beef and Capellini pasta. Incredible dining experience. Crafted cocktails and specially baked desserts. **Note:** Reservations should be made months in advance if you hope to get a table.

OYSTER BAH
1962 N Halsted St, Chicago, 773-248-3000
www.oysterbah.com
CUISINE: Seafood
DRINKS: Full Bar
SERVING: Dinner; Lunch added Fri - Sun
PRICE RANGE: $$$
NEIGHBORHOOD: Lincoln Park
Here the menu focuses of fresh seafood including a mixture of classic and unique seafood dishes. Don't let the cute name throw you, or the tablecloths with the New England red checkerboard design. Or the

nautical do-dads decorating the place. This place has great food. Thy usually offer 8 types of oysters, and you can have them fried, raw, grilled or broiled. I've had them each way and they are all excellent. Other menu favorites: One-Sided Snapper, Stuffed Clam dish baked with chorizo. Small wine and cocktail list.

PARACHUTE
3500 N Elston Ave, 773-654-1460
www.parachuterestaurant.com
CUISINE: Korean
DRINKS: Full Bar
SERVING: Dinner
PRICE RANGE: $$$
NEIGHBORHOOD: North Side
Trendy eatery with red brick walls and low lighting (at night) help to project a friendly, even cozy ambience. Has a menu of creative Korean-American fare. Favorites: Pork Katsu with Napa cabbage; Dolsot bibimbap (with yellowfin tuna, smoked onion & lima beans); Ddukbokki (with pork and peach sofrito); and Broiled whole trout unagi style. Vegetarian and Gluten-free options.

PARSON'S CHICKEN & FISH
2952 W Armitage St, Chicago, 773-384-3333
www.parsonschickenandfish.com
CUISINE: American
DRINKS: Full Bar
SERVING: Lunch & Dinner
PRICE RANGE: $
NEIGHBORHOOD: Logan Square
Absolutely nothing fancy about this popular take-out
spot selling fried chicken and fish. You can sit inside
or outside. The grilled chicken is cooked Amish style
(with citrus, scallions, rum, Habanero and spices),
and you can get 2 pieces, a half chicken or a whole
one. The fish fry comes with 3 piece, 6 pieces, or 9.
The fish sandwich, however, is better, and comes
with beer-battered fish, cole slaw and American
cheese. (Get a side order of hush puppies.)

PASSEROTTO
5420 N Clark St, 708-607-2102
www.passerottochicago.com
CUISINE: Korean

DRINKS: Full Bar
SERVING: Dinner, Closed Sun & Mon
PRICE RANGE: $$$
NEIGHBORHOOD: Andersonville
Hip though still very casual eatery attracting a trendy crowd to its sleek interior with subdued lighting offering a menu of Korean fare with a few Italian influences. Four-course prix-fixe menu which is a good idea if you're not familiar with Korean cuisine. Favorites: Korean style tartare (rhubarb & white anchovies); Ddukbokki Lamb Neck Ragu with rice cakes; Kalbi Glazed Short Ribs & kimchi; Spare Ribs; Pork tenderloin.

PRIME & PROVISIONS
222 N La Salle St, Chicago, 312-726-7777
www.primeandprovisions.com

CUISINE: Steakhouse/Seafood/American (Traditional)
DRINKS: Full Bar
SERVING: Lunch & Dinner; Dinner only on Sat; closed Sun
PRICE RANGE: $$$$
NEIGHBORHOOD: The Loop
Located in a nearly 100-year-old building, this popular eatery celebrates true steakhouse cuisine. They dry-age the meat here on site. Great place for meat lovers looking for a great rib eye, Porterhouse, filet or steak. The bone-in Porterhouse for 2 costs over $100, but it's sure worth it. While they have all the usual steakhouse items, they have a few twists worthy of attention, like the crispy skinned fried chicken or the thick-cut bacon that looks more like a little pork chop than bacon. Great cocktails. Reservations recommended. Dessert? You gotta go for the banana cream pie.

PROST
2566 N Lincoln Ave, Chicago, 773-880-9900
www.prostchi.com
CUISINE: German/American Traditional
DRINKS: Full Bar
SERVING: Dinner, Lunch on Fri - Sun
PRICE RANGE: $$
NEIGHBORHOOD: Lincoln Park, DePaul
If you've ever been to a classic Bräuhaus in Munich, you'll feel right at home in this place in Lincoln Park. Typical German beer hall with a menu of traditional German fare. Great selection of beers including 24

draft beers (all German). Lots of TVs for sports fans. Try the Giant pretzel (enough for 4 to share).

PUB ROYALE
2049 W Division St, Chicago, 773-661-6874
www.pubroyale.com
CUISINE: Anglo/Indian
DRINKS: Full Bar
SERVING: Dinner; Lunch Fri - Sun
PRICE RANGE: $$
NEIGHBORHOOD: West Town – Wicker Park
Great pub with an impressive selection of tap beers and ciders. Despite the name "pub," it's known for excellent craft cocktails, and especially its "Royale Cups," their take on old standards like Pimm's Cup. Very refreshing drinks, all of them (like the Tipple Royale Cup No. 1, which includes cucumber, strawberry, ginger beer & of course, that great drink that without which there would have been no Empire at all, Gin. Menu of Anglo-Indian pub fare including interesting dishes like eggplant curry, lamb dumplings, and chicken tikka roll. Great choice for weekend brunch.

THE PUBLICAN
837 W Fulton Market St, Chicago, 312-733-9555
www.thepublicanrestaurant.com
CUISINE: American
DRINKS: Full Bar
SERVING: Lunch (but late, opens at 3:30) & dinner nightly; weekend brunch from 10
PRICE RANGE: $$$

NEIGHBORHOOD: Fulton Market, Near West Side, West Loop

Known in these parts for their oysters, carefully selected pork, and beer. The menu is very much seasonal. Expect items like wild king salmon roe, smoked arctic char, duck hearts (with kale marmalade), blood sausages (among the best I've had), sucking pig, porchetta. There's even a daily pickle selection. They have a grilled chicken sauced with *piri piri* chile. He salts down the chicken a day before it's cooked, which makes it retain juices. Mouth-watering. They have a sticky bun bread pudding for dessert that's different and pleasing.

-This Little Piggy-
Winter food at The Purple Pig, Chicago

THE PURPLE PIG
444 N Michigan Ave, Chicago, 312-464-1744
www.thepurplepigchicago.com
CUISINE: Tapas/Mediterranean
DRINKS: Full Bar
SERVING: Lunch, Dinner
PRICE RANGE: $$
NEIGHBORHOOD: Near North Side

This is an intimate gastropub run by Jimmy Bannos Jr offering a tasting adventure for foodies. Here you'll find dishes you won't find anywhere else. Menu favorites include: Milk braised pork shoulder and Pork neck bone gravy with ricotta. There's also a great wine list and impressive offering of beers. Usually a long wait for tables. No reservations.

ROISTER
951 W Fulton Market, Chicago, 312-491-0058
www.roisterrestaurant.com
CUISINE: American (New)
DRINKS: Full bar
SERVING: Lunch & Dinner
PRICE RANGE: $$$
NEIGHBORHOOD: Fulton Market, Near West Side, West Loop
Located in the Fulton Market area, this hip eatery offers a menu of creative New American cuisine. This place has an unabashedly fun feel to it. Your flatware is tucked into a little pouch that will remind you of that "mess kit" you had when you went camping as a kid. The plates were crafted by a nearby an Illinois firm, Eshelman Pottery. The music played here started with a list of 900 songs sent in by everybody, but now they have about 3,000 songs. Favorites: Pasta & clams and Baked lasagna. Creative desserts.

RUSSIAN TEA TIME
77 E Adams St, Chicago, 312-360-0000
www.russianteatime.com
CUISINE: Russian
DRINKS: Full Bar
SERVING: Lunch, Dinner
PRICE RANGE: $$$
NEIGHBORHOOD: The Loop
One visit to this landmark Russian restaurant and
you'll feel like part of the family. (Well, it might take
two visits.) Typical Russian fare like Beef Stroganoff,
Chicken Roulette, Ukrainian borscht, herring. Other
regional cuisines represented are Uzbek, Azerbaijani
and Moldavian. The Tea Service itself offers over 30
different teas, but that's not as important as the
unusual pastries, sweets and other savories you get to
choose from, including rugelach and Pozharski
croquettes. Don't overlook the "vodka flights" that

include various flavored vodkas. The wine selection, as you can imagine in a place like this, is wide ranging and carries labels you've never heard of.

SCHWA
1466 N Ashland Ave, Chicago, 773-252-1466
www.schwarestaurant.com
CUISINE: American
DRINKS: No Booze
SERVING: Dinner
PRICE RANGE: $$$$
NEIGHBORHOOD: Wicker Park
Here fine cuisine becomes a dining experience. Chef Michael Carlson serves up a menu of vivid courses featuring seasonal ingredients from around the world. A nine-course meal here is an unforgettable experience. Check out the tasting menu.

SIBLING'S SOUL FOOD
8127 S Ashland Ave, Chicago, 773-892-1078

https://www.allmenus.com/il/chicago/352006-morrisons-soul-food/menu/
CUISINE: Soul Food
DRINKS: No Booze
SERVING: Lunch, Dinner
PRICE RANGE: $$ / **cash only**
NEIGHBORHOOD: Auburn Gresham
Fair choice for comfort food like Mac 'n Cheese, ribs and cornbread. Daily specials. You go down a cafeteria line and point to the dishes you want. Just like the old days. Food iso only fair, not great. Avoid Sunday (unless you want to see everybody dressed to the nines), because you run into the after-church crowd. Cash only.

SHAW'S CRAB HOUSE
21 E Hubbard St, Chicago, 312-527-2722
www.shawscrabhouse.com
CUISINE: Seafood, Sushi Bar
DRINKS: Full Bar
SERVING: Lunch, Dinner
PRICE RANGE: $$$
NEIGHBORHOOD: Near North Side
Shaw's is actually two restaurants in one – a sophisticated seafood restaurant and an energetic oyster bar. Both offer a menu featuring top-grade fish and shellfish, oysters, and sushi and sashimi combinations. Menu favorites include the Maryland crab cake and the oysters (East and West Coast varieties). Bustling happy hour.

THE SMOKE DADDY
1804 W Division St, Chicago, 773-772-6656

www.thesmokedaddy.com
CUISINE: Barbeque
DRINKS: Full Bar
SERVING: Lunch, Dinner
PRICE RANGE: $$
NEIGHBORHOOD: Wicker Park
Barbecue sandwiches, down-home specials, and really loud music. Old time barbeque joint that serves barbeque chicken and pork, down-home specials, ribs, mac 'n cheese and even has a veggie burger. Interesting cocktails like the Bloody Mary garnished with meat. Live music. Known for its world famous Chicago BBQ sauce.

SMYTH AND THE LOYALIST
177 N Ada St. Ste 001, Chicago, 773-913-3773
www.smythandtheloyalist.com
CUISINE: American (New)/Seafood
DRINKS: Full Bar
SERVING: Dinner; closed Sun & Mon
PRICE RANGE: $$
NEIGHBORHOOD: Near West Side, West Loop
There are two distinct eateries here. Casual dining downstairs in what is called the Loyalist Pub, where you can get excellent pub grub like Burgers & Fries and Chicken wings. The burgers have bacon worked into the patties, so they're really delicious. You'll find the Loyalist Pub crowded after work as people pour in to relax. Upstairs at Smyth's you get 3 tasting menus (5, 8 and 12 courses) to choose from in a much fancier setting. The produce is grown specifically for these two restaurants. Impressive selection of craft cocktails, craft beers and wines.

SOUTHPORT GROCERY & CAFÉ

3552 N Southport Ave, (betw. Addison St & Eddy St), Chicago, 773-665-0100

www.southportgrocery.com

CUISINE: American

DRINKS: Full bar

SERVING: Breakfast & Lunch (sometimes does dinner, but usually only Thursday and Friday—check to be sure)

PRICE RANGE: $$

NEIGHBORHOOD: Lakeview

A pioneer of the restaurant-plus-market concept, the chef and owner, Lisa Santos, still does it right. The airy, bright dining room has booth tables along the side wall and the staff's market picks on the blackboard: pork belly with Fat Toad Farm goat

milk caramel sauce from Vermont, feta from nearby Prairie Pure Farm. The eclectic menu is strong in grown-up kids' fare -- cupcake pancakes, stuffed

French toast, grilled Brie sandwiches, artisanal Italian sodas -- and starred items are available in the grocery. Ms. Santos's kitchen also makes and packages a line of products for the market, including bread pudding pancake mix, granola and blueberry preserves.

SUPERDAWG DRIVE-IN
6363 N Milwaukee Ave, Chicago, 773-763-0660
www.superdawg.com
CUISINE: Hot dogs, Hamburgers
DRINKS: No Booze
SERVING: Lunch & Dinner
PRICE RANGE: $
NEIGHBORHOOD: Norwood Park
This is an iconic hot dog drive-in. Really fun to come here. They make their own hot dogs and serve piping hot fries that are out of this world. Everything on the menu is tasty but not if you're counting calories. The malts are the best. This is a drive-in. Limited indoor standing space. There are picnic tables when the weather is nice.

SUPERKHANA INTERNATIONAL
3059 W Diversey Ave, 773-661-9028
www.superkhanachicago.com
CUISINE: Indian/American (New)
DRINKS: Full Bar
SERVING: Dinner, Closed Sun & Mon.
PRICE RANGE: $$
NEIGHBORHOOD: Logan Square
Trendy eatery with nice textures used in the interior design, from the stone walls to the slanted wide beamed light wood ceiling to the open-air patio out

back, all very nice. Offers an American twist on Indian street food. Favorites: Achaari Pork Pao and Butter Chicken Supreme. Lots of Vegetarian options here. Reservations recommended.

TAC QUICK THAI KITCHEN
1011 W Irving Park Rd, Chicago, 773-327-5253
www.tacquick.com
CUISINE: Thai
DRINKS: No Booze
SERVING: Lunch & Dinner
PRICE RANGE: $$
NEIGHBORHOOD: Wrigleyville
This top-notch Thai eatery features a creative menu with dishes like cookie-cutter curries and pad thais. Ask for the second menu where you'll discover items like the tart and smoky pork and rice sausage and ground chicken with crispy basil and preserved eggs. Check out the specials.

TANGO SUR
3763 N Southport Ave, Chicago, 773-477-5466
www.tangosur.net
CUISINE: Steakhouse; Argentine
DRINKS: No Booze; BYOB (no corkage fee)
SERVING: Dinner
PRICE RANGE: $$
NEIGHBORHOOD: Lakeview
This family-style Argentinean steakhouse, with two dining areas, serves delicious steaks. Large portions. They have no alcohol but have a no corkage BYOB policy. Menu favorites include: Empanadas and Melted provolone served with red peppers; sliced

eggplant served in vinegar; breaded beef Milanesa with 2 fried eggs on top; churrasco steaks, grilled half chicken; grilled short ribs served with sausages. Very busy and there's usually a wait.

TERZO PIANO
159 E Monroe St, Chicago, 312-443-8650
www.terzopianochicago.com
CUISINE: Italian
DRINKS: Full Bar
SERVING: Lunch
PRICE RANGE: $$$
NEIGHBORHOOD: The Loop
Located in the new Modern Wing of the Art Institute of Chicago, this is a great place for lunch or Sunday Brunch. Chef Tony Mantuano, known for his four-star Italian restaurant Spiaggia, uses fresh, organic, and sustainably produced ingredients for his seasonal menus. Menu favorites include: Margherita pizza and Sausage flatbread. Nice wine list.

TRY OUR FAMOUS

FILIPINO BREAKFAST

LONGANIZA		*9.95*
Sweet anise-wine chorizo sausage		
TOCINO		*9.95*
Annato and anise cured pork shoulder		
TOCINO + LONGANIZA		*9.95*
BANGUS	BABY *9.95* BIGATIN	*14.95*
Boneless grilled milkfish		
SPAM [HOT & SPICY]		*9.25*
SKIRT STEAK	HALF *14.50* FULL	*16.95*
PORK CHOP	HALF *12.95* FULL	*14.95*

Fresh Lugao
EVERYDAY

UNCLE MIKE'S PLACE
1700 W Grand Ave, Chicago, 312-226-5318
www.unclemikesplace.com
CUISINE: American/Filipino
DRINKS: No Booze
SERVING: Breakfast, Lunch
PRICE RANGE: $$
NEIGHBORHOOD: Ukrainian Village, West Town
Comfortable no-frills eatery. Menu offers all-day-breakfast and lunch. Their classic BLT is one of the best in town. Best Filipino breakfast food in Chicago. Try the Tocino and Bangus. Or the lugao, which is chicken and rice soup. They have a dish with spam and garlic rice that sounds terrible, but tastes great. Tea is free with your meal. The people here are very conscientious, and if you don't come back for the

food, which you will, you will definitely want to visit these people again.

WHEREWITHALL
3472 N Elston Ave, 773-692-2192
www.wherewithallchi.com
CUISINE: American (New)
DRINKS: Full Bar
SERVING: Lunch, Dinner, Late night
PRICE RANGE: $$$
NEIGHBORHOOD: Avondale
Distressed ceiling gives the place a lot of character. Small intimate space is quite fun & charming. The little patio out back is very nice, with its red brick wall and tilted fencing. This popular eatery offera a prix-fixe menu of 4-courses of New American fare. Favorites: Fresh trout and Skirt steak, but you never know what they'll serve till you get there. Nice wine pairings. I'd advise reserving ahead (for a table) because it's so small, but the bar doesn't take reservations, so you might try just walking in.

XOCO
449 N Clark St, Chicago, 312-661-1434
www.rickbayless.com
CUISINE: Mexican
DRINKS: Beer & Wine Only
SERVING: Lunch & Dinner; closed Sunday and Monday
PRICE RANGE: $$
NEIGHBORHOOD: Near North Side
Rick Bayless has a mini restaurant empire here in Chicago, and this is one of his stars. It's not fast food

Mexican, but rapid enough to be confused as fast food. No question that it's good: churros fresh from the fryer. Empanada, Mexican hot chocolate (they grind the Mexican cacao beans in the front window), tortas (Mexican sub sandwiches), caldos (meal-in-a-bowl soups with veggies, seafood or pork belly). Only seats 40 and they don't take reservations, so plan on going early or late.

NIGHTLIFE

ALLIUM RESTAURANT AND BAR CHICAGO
Four Seasons Hotel
120 E Delaware Pl, Chicago, 312-799-4900
www.alliumchicago.com
CUISINE: American
DRINKS: Full Bar
SERVING: Breakfast, Lunch, Dinner
PRICE RANGE: $$$
NEIGHBORHOOD: Near North Side
This is one of those classy hotel bars serving creative
cocktails. If you get hungry there is a snack menu that

includes tasty treats like: Mushrooms n' Toast, Crispy Brussels Sprouts and Roasted Carrots.

THE AVIARY
955 W Fulton Market St, Chicago, 312-226-0868
www.theaviary.com
NEIGHBORHOOD: Fulton Market, Near West Side, West Loop
If you think you can just saunter up to the bar at the Aviary, think again. A limited number of reservations are accepted each day for seatings at 6, 8 and 10 p.m. Would-be patrons must e-mail their requests to reservations@theaviary.com. If selected, you will be contacted by 4 p.m. the day of the reservation. So much for advance planning. Owned by Chef Grant Achatz and his partner, Nick Kokonas, owners of celebrated Chicago restaurants like Alinea, this bar offers specialty cocktails that you won't find anywhere else, like the Tropic Thunder served in a specially designed glass called the porthole. Another specialty cocktail called the Ford's Model Tea Party is made with Ford's gin, Old Pulteney Scotch and Atsby Armadillo Cake vermouth, Mandarine Napoleon and Sicilian blood orange tea and is served in a china cup. Great list of beers from small brewers. A must-see for cocktail lovers.

BIG CHICKS
5024 N Sheridan Rd, (bet. Argyle St & Carmen Ave),
Chicago, 773-728-5511
www.bigchicks.com
NEIGHBORHOOD: Uptown
There are so many clubs on Ontario Street, just north
of the Loop, that it's sometimes known as Red Bull
Row. To ease out of a troubled day, go to Big Chicks,
a gay bar that welcomes everyone. The drinks are
cheap, the crowd is friendly and the décor is nicely
weird.

BILLY SUNDAY
3143 West Logan Blvd, Chicago, 773-661-2485

www.billy-sunday.com
NEIGHBORHOOD: Logan Square
A dark and charming craft-cocktail joint that serves creative cocktails befitting a chemist. Antique china and chandeliers make you feel like you're back in the 19th Century. There's also a delightful menu of excellent food.

BUDDY GUY'S LEGENDS
700 S. Wabash, Chicago, 312-427-1190
www.buddyguy.com
NEIGHBORHOOD: South Loop
Known as the nation's premier blues club, this club offers an impressive roster of local, national, and international blues acts. Some of the talents that have performed here include: Van Morrison, Willie Dixon, The Rolling Stones, Lou Rawls, David Bowie, John Mayer, Stevie Ray Vaughan, and The Pointer Sisters. Buddy Guy takes the stage every January with a series of sold out shows. Open 7 nights a week. Southern Cajun soul food menu available. Check website for schedule and prices.

CALIFORNIA CLIPPER BAR
1002 N California Ave, Chicago, 773-384-2547
www.californiaclipper.com
NEIGHBORHOOD: Humboldt Park
This is a restored cocktail lounge that's out of another era. Here you'll find board games instead of TVs. Chicago's only bar with grape soda in the gun. Live music Fridays and Saturdays. Monday night is Trivia Night. Cash only.

CH DISTILLERY & COCKTAIL BAR
564 W Randolph St, Chicago, 312-707-8780
www.chdistillery.com
NEIGHBORHOOD: Near West Side, West Loop
Distillery that also has a bar with a menu of shared
plates like Duck tacos and Chicken wings. Here they
distill vodka, gin, whiskey, bourbon and a few others.
You can see the shining stills behind a glass wall.
Crafted cocktails are created from their products.
Tours available. This is a no-tip bar.

CHARLIE'S CHICAGO
3726 N Broadway St, Chicago, 773-871-8887
www.charlieschicago.com
NEIGHBORHOOD: Lakeview
Gay country themed dance club with the best in
entertainment, 7 days a week. Charlie's Chicago
offers a roster that includes: award-winning country
programming, after-hours dance party, Bingo,
Karaoke, and free dance lessons. Resident & Guest
DJs and light shows. Open until 4 a.m. Cover charge.

THE CLOSET
3325 N Broadway St, Chicago, 773-477-8533
www.theclosetchicago.com
NEIGHBORHOOD: Lakeview
Open since 1978, this neighborhood bar, although
known as a lesbian bar, welcomes everyone. A
friendly joint with games like darts and video
bowling. Free Wi-Fi. TVs feature sports and music
videos. Karaoke on Thursday nights. Theme parties.

THE COMEDY BAR
500 N LaSalle Blvd, Chicago, 312 836 0499
www.comedybar.com/chicago/
NEIGHBORHOOD: Near North Side, River North
It offers performances on Fridays and Saturdays at 8
and 10 p.m. You won't find big names, but a hit-or-
miss roster of itinerant comedians, some who heckle
the audience in language that can't be printed here.
Modest cover includes admission to the upstairs
lounge, where bottle-service vodkas run $200 or
more.

DRUMBAR at RAFFAELLO HOTEL
201 E Delaware Pl, Chicago, 312-933-4805
www.drumbar.com
NEIGHBORHOOD: Near North Side
Located on top of the **Raffaello Hotel**, this popular
rooftop bar offers a menu of creative cocktails.
There's an intimate indoor lounge and an outdoor
terrace that offers beautiful views of Lake Michigan.

ELIXIR

3452 N Halsted, (bet. Newport Ave & Cornelia Ave), Chicago, 773-975-9244

www.elixirchicago.com

NEIGHBORHOOD: Lakeview

In Boystown, where you can easily find a place to sing show tunes, dance or screen "RuPaul's Drag Race," Elixir is a nice spot to relax. Specialty cocktails are big here.

EMPTY BOTTLE

1035 N Western Ave, Chicago, 773-276-3600

www.emptybottle.com

NEIGHBORHOOD: Ukrainian Village

This popular live music venue offers a schedule of local and independent music. Avant-garde bands play late at night, but Friday nights have morphed into a kind of country honky-tonk scene. Cash only. Menu features some great local breweries. It's a bit divey but friendly.

HAYMARKET PUB & BREWERY

737 W Randolph St, Chicago, 312-638-0700

www.haymarketbrewing.com

NEIGHBORHOOD: Near West Side

This pub features two separate areas – one for the bar and the other for dining. Guests can actually see the fermentation room where the beer is made. This place attracts an interesting crowd as it's the home of Chicago's Drinking & Writing Theater. Great beer selection with over 30 on tap. Appetizer menu available.

THE HIDEOUT

1354 W Wabansia Ave, Chicago, 773-227-4433

www.hideoutchicago.com

NEIGHBORHOOD: Noble Square

Open since 1934, this small music venue that looks like a dive bar is very prominent in Chicago's live music scene and offers a schedule of live music, theatrical performances, dance parties and comedy shows. Billed as "a regular guy bar for irregular folks who just don't fit in." Artists who have played here include Neko Case, Wilco and Mavis Staples. Check website for schedule.

HOUSE OF BLUES

329 N Dearborn St, Chicago, 312-923-2000

www.houseofblues.com/chicago

NEIGHBORHOOD: Near North Side

Whether you want a gospel brunch or a late-night jam fest, it's worth checking the schedule at House of

Blues Chicago, which has featured artists like the Who and Al Green. Popular music venue with locations all over the U.S. This venue attracts big-name performers from all genres including jazz, blues, gospel, alternative rock and hop-hop. Interior is a mix of blues bar and opera house. There's a second-stage in the restaurant offering live blues nightly. Check out the popular Sunday gospel brunch.

HYDRATE
3458 N Halsted St, Chicago, 773-975-9244
www.hydratechicago.com
NEIGHBORHOOD: Lakeview
Known as Chicago's Premier Gay Dance Club, offers a fun night featuring theme nights, drag shows and dancers. Cover Charge. Open 7 nights.

JAZZ SHOWCASE
806 S Plymouth Ct, Chicago, 312-360-0234
www.jazzshowcase.com
NEIGHBORHOOD: South Loop
Founded in 1947 by Joe Segal, this is the oldest jazz club in Chicago. The 170-seat venue offers a roster of some of the best jazz acts in Chicago. Some of the greats who have performed here include: Chris Potter, Frank Morgan, James Carter, Stu Katz, McCoy Tyner, Dexter Gordon, Richie Cole, Dizzy Gillespie, George Benson, and Joe Farrell. Check website for schedule and prices. Cover charge.

MILK ROOM
12 S Michigan Ave, Chicago, 312-792-3535
www.milkroomchicago.com

NEIGHBORHOOD: The Loop
Popular bar for fans of well-crafted cocktails made with unusual and rare ingredients. It's on the second floor of the Chicago athletic Association Hotel. Only 8 stools in here, and you have to reserve one. VERY expensive. Popular drinks: Old Scout Old Fashioned and the Whiskey Sour Redemption.

MURPHY'S BLEACHERS

3655 N Sheffield St (between Addison St & Waveland Ave), Chicago, 773-281-5356
www.murphysbleachers.com
NEIGHBORHOOD: Wrigleyville, Lakeview
Founded in the 1930s as Ernie's Bleachers, a hot dog stand hawking beer by the pail, Murphy's Bleachers is now a perpetually packed sports bar across the street from -- what else? -- the bleachers at Wrigley Field. Never mind that the Cubs haven't won a World Series since 1908. You can enjoy beers with the throngs who love them anyway.

REPLAY BEER & BOURBON

3439 N Halsted St, Chicago, 773-661-9632
www.replaylakeview.com
NEIGHBORHOOD: Boystown
Popular gay bar with a nice outdoor patio. Fills up late. Retro-feel with bar TVs, video games, jukebox and free popcorn. 25 beers on tap.

ROOF ON THE WIT
201 N State St, Chicago, 201 N State St, Chicago,
312 239 9502
www.thewithotel.com
NEIGHBORHOOD: The Loop
Upscale rooftop lounge located on the 27th floor of
the Wit Hotel. Great summer scene. Creative
cocktails and snack menu. Great spot for a first date
when the weather permits.

ROSA'S LOUNGE
3420 W Armitage Ave, Chicago, 773-342-0452
www.rosaslounge.com
NEIGHBORHOOD: Logan Square
A family-owned blues lounge that features a variety
of styles showcasing legendary singers like David
Honeyboy Edwards, Homesick James and Pinetop.

ROSCOE'S
3356 N Halsted St, Chicago, 773-281-3355

www.roscoes.com
NEIGHBORHOOD: Lakeview
Since 1987, Roscoe's has been entertaining crowds.
By day, it's a neighborhood bar with a sidewalk café
but by night Roscoe's transforms into a lively
nightclub with a great dance floor. Theme nights,
drag shows, boy dancers, and Karaoke on Mondays &
Wednesdays. Cover charge.

SCOFFLAW
3201 W Armitage Ave, Chicago, 773-252-9700
www.scofflawchicago.com
NEIGHBORHOOD: Logan Square
A popular neighborhood bar that serves great
cocktails like Sly Devil made with Scofflaw Old Tom
gin. The food is good too, particularly the burgers.
There are tables but they're hard to come by and
there's always a wait.

SIMON'S
5210 N Clark St, Chicago, 773-878-0894

NEIGHBORHOOD: Andersonville/Uptown
One of Chicago's old time favorite dive bars. Ok beer selection on tap and good Glogg. Juke box for music. Cash only.

SIDETRACK
3349 N Halsted St, Chicago, 773-477-9189
www.sidetrackchicago.com
NEIGHBORHOOD: Lakeview
A large gay video bar with five different bar areas on two-levels including a deck bar. Show tunes on the big screen, sing-along nights. Friendly crowd and staff.

THE VIOLET HOUR
1520 N Damen Ave, Chicago, 773-252-1500
www.theviolethour.com

NEIGHBORHOOD: Wicker Park
This cocktail lounge may be difficult to find as there's no sign but it's worth the search. Inside there's a sign requesting that you refrain from using your cell phone. The décor is interesting with crystal chandeliers and beautiful hardwood floors giving the space a ballroom feel. The classic cocktails served are delish and strong but slow to come as the bartenders take great care in the preparation. Great atmosphere for drinking with friends.

WEEGEE'S LOUNGE
3659 W Armitage Ave, Chicago, 773-384-0707
www.weegeeslounge.com
NEIGHBORHOOD: Logan Square
An old-school cocktail lounge that does things their way, like making their own sour mix and ginger syrup. Here you'll find an impressive menu of beers (more than 100) with many coming from small

brewers. The bar is known for its glamorous, yet potent cocktails like the Aviation made from gin, fresh lemon juice, crème de violette and Luxardo maraschino liqueur. The bar also serves classic tunes ranging from Glenn Miller to Memphis Slim.

INDEX

82

WANT 3 **FREE** THRILLERS?

Why, of course you do!

If you like these writers--
Vince Flynn, Brad Thor, Tom Clancy, James Patterson,
David Baldacci, John Grisham, Brad Meltzer, Daniel
Silva, Don DeLillo

If you like these TV series –
House of Cards, Scandal, West Wing, The Good Wife,
Madam Secretary, Designated Survivor

You'll love the **unputdownable** series about
Jack Houston St. Clair, with political intrigue, romance,
suspense.

Besides writing travel books, I've written political thrillers
for many years that have delighted hundreds of thousands
of readers. I want to introduce you to my work!
Send me an email and I'll send you a link where you can
download the first 3 books in my bestselling series,
absolutely FREE.

Mention **this book** when you email me.

andrewdelaplaine@mac.com

CPSIA information can be obtained
at www.ICGtesting.com
Printed in the USA
BVHW041313291221
625055BV00018B/1786